Extreme Cars

SPORTS CARS

Steve Rendle

PowerKiDS press

New York

Published in 2022 by The Rosen Publishing Group, Inc.
29 East 21st Street, New York, NY 10010

Originally Published in English by Haynes Publishing under the title: Extreme Cars Pocket Manual © Haynes Publishing 2019

Cataloging-in-Publication Data
Names: Rendle, Steve.
Title: Sports cars / Steve Rendle.
Description: New York : PowerKids Press, 2022. | Series: Extreme cars | Includes glossary and index.
Identifiers: ISBN 9781725332492 (pbk.) | ISBN 9781725332515 (library bound) | ISBN 9781725332508 (6 pack) | ISBN 9781725332522 (ebook)
Subjects: LCSH: Sports cars--Juvenile literature.
Classification: LCC TL236.R448 2022 | DDC 629.228--dc23

Design by Richard Parsons and James Robertson

The following agencies have given permission to use their images:

Photographs supplied by the individual car manufacturers.
Additional images published with the permission of Getty.
Cover, Glebiy/Shutterstock.com; Cover, p. 1 Double Brain/Shutterstock.com; pp. 3-5, 8, 9, 12, 13, 16, 17, 20, 21, 24, 25, 28-32 Carlos Caetano/Shutterstock.com.

Manufactured in the United States of America

CPSIA Compliance Information: Batch #CWPK22. For Further Information contact Rosen Publishing, New York, New York at 1-800-237-9932.

CONTENTS

INTRODUCTION

This book is about sports cars, and we've picked some of the most extreme ones in the world. You might wonder what made us select some but not others. Well, for a start, all the cars in this book have been, or will be, available to buy, as long as buyers have enough money and, in some cases, if they meet the conditions that the car manufacturer sets. You won't see these cars every day—and there are some that you will probably never see—but they are all out there on the world's roads or tracks somewhere!

Most of the cars are very modern and fitted with the latest technology. There are a few older cars too. However old they are, though, all the cars included have been selected because they are built to provide an incredible experience for the driver—but not necessarily for passengers. In most cases, the cars need a skilled driver to make the most of them. Some are racing cars for the road, while others are road cars that were built so that they could also be raced.

Every one of the cars included has extreme performance—either top speed or acceleration—and most are able to corner like racing cars. Of course, they all sound incredible. Some have road-car luxuries too, such as leather trim, in-car entertainment, air conditioning, and satnav.

Perhaps one day you might be lucky enough to get behind the wheel of one of the ultimate machines featured in the following pages and find out just how exciting they can be. Until then, enjoy reading and daydreaming about them!

ABBREVIATIONS AND THEIR MEANINGS

bhp	brake horsepower—available power of an engine
cc	cubic centimeters—volume of engine cylinders added together
in	inches—used for wheel sizes
kg	kilograms—unit of weight
kph	kilometers per hour—unit of speed
kW	kilowatts—unit of power
lb	pounds—unit of weight
lb ft	pound foot—unit of torque
LCD	liquid-crystal display
mm	millimeters—unit of length
mph	miles per hour—unit of speed
Nm	newton meter—unit of torque
rpm	revolutions per minute—the number of turns in one minute
s	seconds—unit of time
V6	V-shaped engine with six cylinders (three on each side of the "V")
V8	V-shaped engine with eight cylinders (four on each side of the "V")
V12	V-shaped engine with 12 cylinders (six on each side of the "V")
W16	W-shaped engine with 16 cylinders (four on each arm of the "W")

ALL ABOUT TIRES

Tires have codes that explain their sizes, and these codes are usually printed on the edge of each tire. As an example, a tire might have a code like **205/50 R15**.

205	means that the tire is 205 mm wide.
50	means that the "profile" (thickness, or height) of the tire is 50 percent of its width. The smaller the number, the thinner the tire.
R	means that the tire is a "radial"-type tire—it is made from layers of material that run in layers at right angles to the direction in which the tire rolls.
15	means that the tire is designed to fit on a 15-in-diameter wheel.

BUGATTI DIVO

A rare and extreme Bugatti built for high-speed cornering

- The car is finished in bare carbon, with gray and "Divo Racing Blue" paint.
- The Divo has 198 lb (90 kg) more downforce than the Chiron.
- Speed is limited to stop the risk of the tires bursting with the extra downforce!
- All 40 cars were sold in one day to owners who had already bought Chirons.

The Bugatti Divo is based on the Bugatti Chiron that replaced the Veyron. Bugatti decided to build the Divo for the company's 110th anniversary in 2019, and only 40 were built. The car is aimed at track use, with racing-car handling and aerodynamics, but is still road-legal. The Divo costs nearly twice as much as a Chiron!

The car is slimmer than the Veyron and Chiron. The front air intake is much bigger, for cooling, and a huge front splitter is featured. The headlights are higher up than other Bugattis and are ultra-slim to leave more space for brake-cooling ducts. A large air duct in the roof guides air toward the big rear wing. The wing is wider than the Chiron's and acts as a huge airbrake by tilting forward when the car is braking. The car is named after Albert Divo, a pilot and mechanic before he won the famous Targa Florio race in Italy twice in the 1920s in a Bugatti Type 35 racing car.

STATISTICS BUGATTI DIVO

Price (new)	$5.8 million
Max speed	Limited to 236 mph (380 kph)
0–62 mph (0–100 kph)	2.4 s
Engine type	64-valve, quad-cam W16, quad turbochargers with intercoolers
Engine capacity	7,993 cc
Max power	1,500 bhp (1,103 kW) at 6,700 rpm
Max torque	1,600 Nm (1,180 lb ft) at 2,000–6,000 rpm
Transmission	7-speed twin-clutch Direct Shift Gearbox (DSG), four-wheel drive, regulated limited-slip differential
Suspension	Double wishbones front and rear
Wheels and tires	20-in front wheels; 21-in rear wheels; 285/30 R20 front tires; 355/25 R21 rear tires
Curb weight	4,323 lb (1,961 kg)
Length	182.7 in (4,641 mm)
Width	79.4 in (2,018 mm)
Height	47.7 in (1,212 mm)
Year introduced	2018

THE DIVO'S COOL REAR LIGHTS ARE PARTLY MADE BY 3D PRINTING.

BUGATTI VEYRON
SUPER SPORT

The Super Sport delivers stunning performance

- The Super Sport's extra power comes from bigger turbochargers.
- The Veyron is named after French Bugatti racing driver Pierre Veyron.
- The Veyron has a total of 10 radiators, including three turbo intercoolers.
- Cristiano Ronaldo, Simon Cowell, and Arnold Schwarzenegger own Veyrons.

The Bugatti Veyron first appeared in 2005 and stunned the car world with its amazing 987-bhp (736 kW) 8.0-liter W12 engine, complete with four turbochargers, and its incredible 253 mph (407 kph) top speed. But this extreme performance comes at a price. A routine service for a Veyron costs $21,000, and a set of four new tires costs over $30,500!

The Veyron was designed and developed by the Volkswagen-Audi group that owns Bugatti and was built in Molsheim, France—the historical home of Bugatti cars. In 2010, Bugatti built 30 Veyron Super Sport models with an uprated engine producing 1,184 bhp (883 kW). In 2013, the Super Sport set a Guinness World Record as the fastest road-legal production car in the world, reaching 268 mph (431 kph), though production versions are limited to a maximum of 258 mph (415 kph). To celebrate the speed record, five Veyron Super Sport World Record Editions were built, with a black carbon body, orange detailing, orange wheels, and the electronic speed limiter removed. A luxury hypercar, it was built for comfort as well as ultimate speed.

STATISTICS BUGATTI VEYRON SUPER SPORT

Price (new)	$2.4 million
Max speed	268 mph (431 kph)
0–62 mph (0–100 kph)	2.5 s
Engine type	64-valve, quad-cam W16, quad turbochargers with intercoolers
Engine capacity	7,993 cc
Max power	1,200 bhp (882 kW) at 6,400 rpm
Max torque	1,500 Nm (1,106 lb ft) at 3,000–5,000 rpm
Transmission	7-speed twin-clutch Direct Shift Gearbox (DSG), four-wheel drive, regulated limited-slip differential
Suspension	Double wishbones front and rear
Wheels and tires	20-in front wheels; 21-in rear wheels; 245/690 R520 front tires; 365/710 R540 rear tires
Curb weight	4,052 lb (1,838 kg)
Length	175.7 in (4,462 mm)
Width	78.7 in (1,998 mm)
Height	47.4 in (1,204 mm)
Year introduced	2010

AT FULL SPEED, A VEYRON COULD ONLY RUN FOR 12 MINUTES ON A FULL TANK!

CATERHAM 620R

The original lightweight sports car with supercharged performance

- The standard 620R carbon seats have no padding.
- Standard and large chassis are available to suit drivers of all shapes and sizes.
- The 620R is the fastest production road car Caterham has ever built.
- The 620S model has 620R performance but also comforts such as a clip-on hood!

The first Caterham 7 appeared in 1973 and was developed from the Lotus 7 designed by legendary F1-car designer Colin Chapman. Over the 45 years since the first Caterham appeared, the cars have become more and more powerful, faster, and slightly crazier, and the 620R is a giant-slayer with its performance!

Colin Chapman designed the Lotus 7 in 1957, and since Caterham began building the car, the basic design has hardly changed. All Caterham models are built for fun and are like grown-up go-karts to drive. The cars are available in kit form for buyers to build themselves or are fully built by the factory. The chassis is tubular steel with aluminum-sheet body panels and glass-fiber nose and wing panels, but the 620R—aimed at track driving but road legal—has a weight-saving carbon-fiber nose and wings, carbon seats, and a carbon dashboard. An immobilizer and removable steering wheel are fitted as standard, but a heater, adjustable leather seats, and a windscreen are optional extras.

STATISTICS CATERHAM 620R

Price (new)	$72,200
Max speed	155 mph (250 kph)
0–62 mph (0–100 kph)	2.8 s
Engine type	Supercharged Ford Duratec 4-cylinder
Engine capacity	1,999 cc
Max power	310 bhp (231 kW) at 7,700 rpm
Max torque	219 Nm (162 lb ft) at 7,350 rpm
Transmission	6-speed sequential gearbox, limited-slip differential
Suspension	Front double wishbones, de Dion rear suspension, adjustable dampers
Wheels and tires	13-in front and rear wheels; 185/55 R13 front tires; 215/55 R13 rear tires
Curb weight	1,345 lb (610 kg)
Length	122 in (3,100 mm)
Width	66.3 in (1,685 mm)
Height	40 in (1,015 mm)
Year introduced	2013

TOP GEAR MAGAZINE CALLED THE 620R "MAD [CRAZY] AS A BOX OF FROGS"!

PORSCHE 911 GT2 RS

The fastest-ever road-going version of a classic sports car

- A built-in titanium roll-cage protects the driver and passenger.
- Cars are available without a sound system and climate-control to save weight.
- Ceramic brake discs reduce weight and improve performance.
- An optional lift system raises the car's front for speed bumps and curbs.

The Porsche 911 first appeared in 1963 and was an instant classic. The 911 GT2 RS was launched in 2017, over 50 years after the first car appeared, and is the quickest and most powerful 911 yet built. Porsche 911s have become more refined over the years, but this version is raw, noisy, and fast!

The huge air intakes at the front of the car cool the engine and brakes, and vents in the hood and front and rear wheel arches let the hot air out, also helping improve the aerodynamics. The car has a lot of weight-saving features, and many of the body parts are made from Carbon-Fiber Reinforced Plastic (CFRP). The roof panel is magnesium, lightweight glass is used, and the twin exhausts are titanium. The catalytic converters glow red at high speeds and, when accelerating hard, can be seen through open holes at the back of the car. Owners can buy a special Porsche Design Chronograph 911 GT2 RS watch, only available to drivers of the 911 GT2 RS!

STATISTICS PORSCHE 911 GT2 RS

Price (new)	$293,200
Max speed	211 mph (340 kph)
0–62 mph (0–100 kph)	2.8 s
Engine type	Twin-turbocharged flat-6
Engine capacity	3,800 cc
Max power	691 bhp (515 kW) at 7,000 rpm
Max torque	750 Nm (553 lb ft) at 2,500–4,500 rpm
Transmission	7-speed double-clutch PDK gearbox, rear-wheel drive
Suspension	McPherson strut front suspension; multi-link rear suspension
Wheels and tires	20-in front wheels; 21-in rear wheels; 265/35 R20 front tires; 325/30 R21 rear tires
Curb weight	3,241 lb (1,470 kg)
Length	179.1 in (4,549 mm)
Width	74 in (1,880 mm)
Height	51.1 in (1,297 mm)
Year introduced	2017

THE CAR IS TOO NOISY TO RACE ON SOME TRACKS AROUND THE WORLD!

SALEEN S7 TWIN TURBO

A thundering V8 supercar built as a racing car, modified for the road

- At 160 mph (257 kph) the aerodynamics produce the car's own weight in downforce.
- S7s have appeared in Hollywood films *Iron Man*, *Bruce Almighty*, and *Redline*.
- Including all racing cars and road models, fewer than 100 S7s have been built.
- The road car has air conditioning, a sound system, and a rear-view camera.

American professional racing driver and businessman Steve Saleen developed the original Saleen S7 for racing back in 2000, and because the racing regulations said the car had to be a production car, a few road cars had to be built. The car doesn't pretend to be refined, and there are no high-tech systems—it is built for speed.

The S7R racing version has been extremely successful, winning races all around the world. The original S7 road car had a normally aspirated engine based on a modified Ford V8, similar to the one used in NASCAR vehicles. The S7 Twin Turbo appeared in 2005, with twin turbochargers and other engine modifications giving an impressive 750 bhp (559 kW). In 2006, a "Competition" package was introduced that included a range of modifications, including improved aerodynamics and suspension and an even more powerful engine giving 1,000 bhp (746 kW). In 2017, Saleen unveiled the S7 Le Mans (LM) to celebrate its success with the racing version of the S7. This limited edition was priced at $1 million and had an uprated 7.0-liter twin-turbo engine producing 1,300 bhp (969 kW)!

STATISTICS SALEEN S7 TWIN TURBO

Price (new)	$585,00
Max speed	248 mph (399 kph)
0–60 mph (0–97 kph)	2.8 s
Engine type	Twin-turbo 16-valve V8
Engine capacity	7.0 liters
Max power	750 bhp (559 kW) at 6,300 rpm
Max torque	949 Nm (700 lb ft) at 4,800 rpm
Transmission	6-speed manual gearbox, limited-slip differential
Suspension	Double wishbones and spring/damper units front and rear
Wheels and tires	19-in front wheels; 20-in rear wheels; 275/35 R19 front tires; 335/30 R20 rear tires
Curb weight	2,967 lb (1,346 kg)
Length	188 in (4,775 mm)
Width	78 in (1,981 mm)
Height	41 in (1,041 mm)
Year introduced	2000

THE SALEEN COMPANY MADE ITS NAME BUILDING MODIFIED FORD MUSTANGS.

W MOTORS FENYR
SUPERSPORT

This wolf-like Supersport looks like it comes from a sci-fi movie

- Three separate active rear wing flaps move automatically.
- A second instrument panel is fitted for the passenger to show speed, rpm, etc.
- The W Motors Fenyr Supersport's doors open rearward.
- The body is made from carbon-fiber and graphene composite.

W Motors is a design company based in Dubai—the first hypercar designer in the Middle East. The "W" in W Motors stands for "Wolf," and the Fenyr Supersport was named after a ferocious wolf from Norse mythology. With its astonishing looks, when Batman needs a new Batmobile, this could be the car!

W Motors was founded in 2012, and the Fenyr Supersport is its second car, following the Lykan Hypersport, also named after a mythical wolf. Only seven Lykan Hypersports were built, and each car had 440 diamonds in the headlights and a holographic display in the cockpit! The Fenyr Supersport first appeared in 2017, and each car is hand-built in Italy. The car is powered by a 3.8-liter twin-turbo flat-6 engine built by specialist tuning company RUF and based on a Porsche engine. The first 10 cars built were "Launch Editions," each finished in a different color scheme featuring bare carbon-fiber. Only 100 cars were expected to be built after the Launch Editions.

STATISTICS W MOTORS FENYR SUPERSPORT

Price (new)	$1.9 million
Max speed	248 mph (400 kph)
0–62 mph (0–100 kph)	2.8 s
Engine type	Porsche-based twin-turbo flat-6
Engine capacity	3,800 cc
Max power	800 bhp (596 kW) at 7,100 rpm
Max torque	980 Nm (723 lb ft) at 4,000 rpm
Transmission	7-speed Porsche dual-clutch PDK gearbox, limited-slip differential
Suspension	Front McPherson struts, rear pushrod-actuated multi-link with horizontal spring/damper units
Wheels and tires	19-in front wheels; 20-in rear wheels; 265/35 R19 front tires; 345/30 R20 rear tires
Curb weight	2,976 lb (1,350 kg)
Length	180.8 in (4,592 mm)
Width	76.2 in (1,935 mm)
Height	47.2 in (1,200 mm)
Year introduced	2017

STANDARD EQUIPMENT INCLUDES A REAR-VIEW CAMERA AND AN INTERNET ROUTER!

GLOSSARY

aerodynamics: having to do with a shape that allows air to flow easily around something so it can move faster

catalytic converter: a vehicle exhaust-system component containing a catalyst which causes conversion of harmful gases into mostly harmless products, such as water and carbon dioxide

chassis: steel tubes that carry the engine, seats, and other parts of a car

dampers: devices in a suspension system that prevent bouncing

differential: a set of gears that transmits engine power to the wheels and allow them to turn at different speeds on turns

hypercar: the most superior and high-performance car on the market

normally aspirated: describing an internal combustion engine in which air intake depends only on atmospheric pressure

radiator: a device that keeps a car engine at an acceptable temperature by passing coolant through water channels that allow heat to be released

satnav: a satellite-based navigation system

suspension: a system of springs and other devices on a car that reduces the shaking and bumping caused by uneven surfaces

torque: a rotating force produced by an engine's crankshaft

transmission: the gear that transmits power from a car or truck's engine to the wheels

FOR MORE INFO

BOOKS

Fishman, Jon M. *Cool Sports Cars*. Minneapolis, MN: Lerner Publications, 2019.

Gish, Ashley. *Sports Cars*. Mankato, MN: Creative Education, 2021.

Lanier, Wendy Hinote. *Sports Cars*. New York, NY: AV2 by Weigl, 2019.

WEBSITES

Sports Cars
www.dkfindout.com/us/transportation/history-cars/sports-cars/
Learn what makes up a sports car and see a diagram of its parts.

Top 50 Best Sports Cars of All Time
blog.dupontregistry.com/news/top-50-best-sports-cars-of-all-time/
Check out this list and see if you agree!

What Makes a Car a Sports Car?
www.jdpower.com/cars/shopping-guides/what-makes-a-car-a-sports-car
Read more about what defines a sports car.

Publisher's note to parents and teachers: Our editors have reviewed the websites listed here to make sure they're suitable for students. However, websites may change frequently. Please note that students should always be supervised when they access the internet.

INDEX